Speak Up

julie! ♥ thank you so much for
supporting me & my book
"Speak up"! I appreciate it so
much!! you are kind & beautiful
wishing you nothing but well
wishes! hope you enjoy the
read :) take care,

erika ♥

Speak Up

Erika Roldan

Life Rattle Press Toronto, Canada

Speak Up

Published by Life Rattle New Writers Series
Life Rattle
Toronto, Canada

ISBN 978-1-987936-68-1

Copy edited by Matthew Famele
Cover and typeset design by Erika Roldan
Illustrations by Caroline Piette

To anyone who has ever been afraid to speak up.

Contents

Writing this book gave me a crap ton of anxiety, loads of sleepless days, and made me challenge myself.

These stories reflect wonderful people in my life, experiences that may have not been the best, and real, raw feels.

I am so happy to share these collection of stories with you.

I am freakin' happy you're alive, that you're able to read, feel, and be here.

take care of yourself,

kuya mike the sunflower ❁

"Holy shit. Haley. Look over there. It's him," I whisper to my sister. It is 9:00 p.m. on a Wednesday evening in February. I squint in his direction, as though the sun were blocking my eyes. I focus on the man sitting at the table in front of us.

We celebrated my sister's twentieth birthday at a seafood restaurant called L.A. Boil in Mississauga, near Winston Churchill. My parents paid for the bill, and as we were about to leave, a couple sat in front of us. I saw his face: thick unruly brows framing his hooded beady black eyes, and spiky hair that stuck up without gel. It has been ten years since I last saw him, but his mischievous smirk remained the same.

I shake Haley's shoulder and point to his booth.

"It's… Tita Maria's son. Kuya Mike. The teacher."

Tita Maria was one of the neighbourhood babysitters from the complex where we lived, when we were younger. She babysat a handful of the kids from the neighbourhood, including my sister, Haley, Melissa from floor seven, and Daniella from townhouse 309. Tita Maria babysat us until we were eight years old. We went over after school every day.

Tita had three sons. Her youngest son was named Michael, who we called Kuya Mike. Kuya Mike was always in his room playing video games when we were over. In Filipino culture, it is respectful to call your elders, "Kuya" or "Ate," meaning older brother and older sister. This is the same for the word, "Tita," meaning aunt.

Kuya Mike would invite Haley, Melissa, Daniella and me to play Xbox in his room after lunch on Wednesdays. His room was small, with only enough space to fit a twin sized bed, a boxed television, and his Xbox. The four of us took turns playing on Kuya Mike's Xbox. If we were lucky, Kuya Mike let one of us sit on his lap, and pushed all the X's and O's on the controller to help one of us win the game. When it was my turn to play, I sat in between his legs, and felt his penis under his basketball shorts, as he wrapped his arms around my shoulders and held the Xbox controller. I let him press the buttons for me so I could beat Haley, Melissa, and Daniella. I wanted to be the winner.

We all had our turn to win the game, only if we sat on Kuya Mike's lap. After playing Xbox, Melissa and I sat in the narrow hallway outside Kuya Mike's room. We giggled about the way Kuya Mike's penis pressed onto our backs. This happened every other day.

When we weren't playing videos games, Tita Maria fed us chicken nuggets and rice. Haley and I sat in the kitchen at a wooden circular table with enough space for two people to sit. Melissa and Daniella sat in the living room beside the kitchen, eating their lunches while watching TVO Kids. Across the kitchen table was the sink where a tray of fruit punch sat.

"Tita Maria, may I drink my glass of fruit punch please?" I asked as I gulped down a spoonful of dry rice. She waddled over, lips straight and said no.

Tita Maria never let us drink juice while we were eating our food. She told us drinking ruins your appetite, and we would be too full to eat our lunches. She told us we can't grow up to be healthy if we didn't eat. I stared at the fruit punch. Condensation trickled down the outside of the plastic cup. I imagined the sweet and tart drink gliding down my throat. I sucked in my cheeks and tried to produce more saliva to swallow the rest of my lunch.

Every summer afternoon, Haley, Melissa and I went to Tita Maria's garden for our favourite afternoon snack: canned tuna and crackers. Her garden was covered in tall, blooming yellow sunflowers. The bright petals stretched across the black prickly center of the flower. The warm wind swept through my fresh-cut bangs that my mom gave me last week. The sun hid behind the murky yellow highrise apartment in front of the complex.

In Tita Maria's garden, there was a grey plastic table with four white plastic chairs around it. A porcelain bowl of tuna sat in the middle of the table, and each of us had our own foil pack of *Skyflakes*. The three of us sat around the table eating our snacks. I cringed while staring at the sunflowers.

The towering sunflowers resembled an eye, staring right back at me. Its black pollen covered the entire flower, and its spikes were like an army of ants. The more I stared at the sunflower, the more I felt the imaginary ants crawling up my arms, tingling the short strands of hair on my forearms and knuckles. I quickly rubbed my arms trying to shake off the imaginary ants.

As we ate our snacks, Tita Maria talked to her

sunflowers while using a pair of scissors to cut off brown, cracked leaves on the stem.

"Tita Maria, how come Daniella's not here today?" I asked.

She did not respond.

Down the sidewalk, I saw Daniella and her mom walking to Tita Maria's sunflower garden. Haley and Melissa shot their hands in the air and waved them side to side to greet Daniella.

"Hi Daniella! You've come to play with us?" yelled Haley.

Daniella's mom stomped her way to Tita's door. She dragged Daniella with her left hand while tears streamed down Daniella's face. I looked at Tita Maria. She stopped chopping off the leaves on her flowers.

"Haley, Melissa, Erika, snack time is over. Go inside with Grandma," said Tita Maria.

Usually after lunch, Tita Maria turned on the television and let us watch Arthur, everyone's favourite show, but today, Tita told us to sit with Grandma and be quiet.

We sat in the living room in front of Grandma as she sat in her creaking rocking chair. We crossed our legs on the living room rug. Behind Grandma's rocking chair were rows of plants and a bunch of handpicked sunflowers hovered over Grandma's left shoulder. The hair on my arms stood up again. Daniella's mom slammed her fist three times on the front door. Tita Maria opened it.

"Maria, I am calling the cops! Daniella tell me your son, Mike, is touching her. She t-t-tell me he touch her p-private," she stuttered.

I never heard Daniella's mom yell before. She always smiled and waved to us whenever she visited Tita Maria.

"What? No Annie! Mike did not do that! He is my son!" Tita shrieked.

"I don't care if he's your son, Maria!" Daniella's mom sobs. "He touch my Daniella. Do you think that's okay? I am calling the cops!" She shook her fist in the air as her voice trembled.

Daniella stood by the door holding her mom's hand. She stared down at the floor, looking at her shoes. She stomped her right foot and watched the soles of her Sketchers light-up shoes flash pink.

"Grandma, what is going on?" Melissa asked.

Grandma smiled at the three of us. Her wrinkled and veiny hand ran through Melissa's curly brown hair.

"Don't you worry. Daniella's mom and Tita are just

having a friendly conversation."

Daniella's mom points her finger at Tita Maria. Tita Maria throws her hands in the air in response.

"I promise you, Annie, Mike would never do this. Let me get him."

We watched Tita Maria walk through the living room, smack her fist on Kuya Mike's door, and kick it open.

"Get out here Mike, Daniella's mom wants to talk to you."

Kuya Mike walked to the front door to talk to Daniella's mom. His basketball shorts swayed against his knees as he walked across the rough carpet, passing us and Grandma. He did not look up or say hi to us.

Daniella's mom curled a fist. "You touch my Daniella! You're going to go to jail."

"What? No I didn't!" yelled Kuya Mike.

"You're a liar!" said Daniella's mom. She stomped away as Tita Maria chased her.

"Please, Annie! Wait, don't do this!" Tita Maria cried. Her voice echoed down the street as she screamed at Daniella's mom to stop. Kuya Mike ran after them. The wind did not budge his black spiky hair as he ran.

For the rest of the afternoon, Grandma turned on the

T.V. and let us watch Arthur, even though Tita Maria said we weren't allowed to. Grandma even brought out more tuna and *Skyflakes* for us to eat. She also brought out the jug of fruit punch and let us drink while we ate. I sipped my fruit punch and sang along to the *Arthur* theme song. The fruit punch tasted just as cold and sweet as I imagined.

"This is the best afternoon ever," I thought.

east side std

It's a Friday night in March. A hostess from East Side Mario's guides Veronica and I to our table near the back of the restaurant. We slip in the red leather booth. The tables around us are empty. A red plaid tablecloth crinkles along the edges of the wooden table. Each table has silverware rolled up in white napkins with red trimmings. A small fake candle sits in the middle of the table — welcoming warmth. The varnished mahogany chair cools the back side of my warm thighs.

Every other Friday night, my friend Veronica and I go to a local restaurant in Mississauga to catch up. We talk about our jobs, the boys that she meets on Tinder, and her latest trips to The Islands. I've known Veronica my whole life. We went to elementary school together. Every day in kindergarten,

Veronica and I would take the bus home together. In Grade 4, I moved to Milton, but we messaged each other on MSN every day. In high school, Veronica and I went to Square One every Friday to check out cute boys and grab food with our parents' money.

I stare at the pictures on the promotions menu, *"crispy Chicken Parmigiana covered in authentic marinara sauce with a side of fresh vegetables and creamy mashed potatoes."*

Our server approaches our table and hands us two glasses of ice water. His narrow face is framed with a pair of silver rectangular glasses matching his silver hoop lip-ring. His hair is gelled with little spikes sticking up.

"Hey, y'all! My name is Michael. I'll be your server for tonight. Have you been to East Side's before?"

"Yes, I have. But this her is first time," I say.

"Awesome! Well, we've got this really great deal going on! It's all-you-can-eat salad and soup with a purchase of any of these entrees." Michael points to the promotional menu that I was looking at.

"…and you get to take home a dish!" He winks.

"Damn, that sounds great," Veronica laughs. She looks up from the menu and stares at me waiting for my reply.

I raise my eyebrow, letting her know I'm down for the deal

too.

"Yeah, we'll get that!" she replies.

Michael chuckles. "Awesome! Great choice!"

After Michael takes our order, he brings us a roll of warm complimentary bread with butter, served on a wooden pan. I break myself a piece and spread on some of the salty and sweet combination. The melted butter lingers on my tongue.

"So, how's that guy that you're seeing?" I ask.

"Who? Evan? Oh, I'm not seeing him anymore. I started seeing another guy from Tinder instead."

"His name is David," she says shoving a piece of bread in her mouth.

She shows me a picture of David. It's a mirror picture of him in a dimmed washroom. He has greasy black hair and his tanned arms bulge under his tight Armani Exchange t-shirt. His lifted shirt exposes his deep v-cut.

I zoom in on David's face, then zoom in on his abs.

"Ou, he's pretty cute."

"Yeah, right? Great in bed too." Veronica winks.

"You're gross," I laugh.

Veronica smiles. "So yeah, anyways, you know how I've been seeing a lot of guys? Well… I really have to tell you something. It's pretty bad."

"Oh, shit. What happened this time?" I flinch.

Usually when Veronica tells me something's wrong, it's about finding out that some guy that she's hooked up from Tinder has a girlfriend or lied about his age.

"Well... um..." Veronica begins.

Michael swings by our table with two large bowls. One bowl of Italian Wedding soup and another of Caesar salad. He places them in the middle of the table.

"Cheers, ladies!"

I grab the red tongs, pile my plate with salad, and think about how to split the five croutons evenly. Veronica spoons herself a few cups of soup.

"So, what were you going to tell me?" I ask.

"Well... I told you I was going to get tested, right?" Veronica plays with her long, box-dyed mahogany hair, staring at her split ends.

"Yeah..." I respond.

"Um, yeah, it's fucked, but I caught something..."

My eyes widen. "Oh fuck..." I try to stay calm and look down at my plate. I continue stabbing my salad.

"Yeah..." she clears her throat.

"Do you know who you got it from? You didn't use a condom?" I ask.

"Well… I asked, like, all those other guys I hooked up with and obviously they said they didn't have anything," Veronica blows on her spoonful of soup. "Bunch of fucking liars," she says.

"What the hell? I wonder which one of them is lying. Probably that guy who cheated on his girl with you, and those other girls."

"Who? Louis? Nah, he showed me a screenshot of his results. So, I literally have no clue who I got it from."

"Fuck… Well, what did you catch?"

I have no idea about the types of STD's that are out there. I've heard of a few of them from watching movies. Like Chlamydia because Coach Carr from *Mean Girls* refers to it, or AIDS because Easy-E from *Straight Outta Compton* had it.

"Yeah… I caught gonorrhea, but don't worry," she smiles. "It's the curable kind, so I won't have it forever. I just gotta take some huge ass horse pills. And you know I can't swallow that shit."

She laughs. Veronica doesn't look up at me throughout our whole conversation. Her eyes stay fixated on her Italian Wedding soup.

Michael turns around the corner of our booth with a few plates on his arms. He puts down the chicken parmesan on Veronica's side of the table and places the sun-dried tomato pasta on my side. Michael comes back with a pepper shaker and a cheese grater.

"Would you like cheese on your pasta?" he asks Veronica.

"Yes please."

"Just say when."

Veronica licks her bottom lip as she watches the grated cheese snowfall on her pasta. The three of us watch the cheese pile on top, hiding the chicken and pasta beneath it.

"Damn, girl! You really love cheese," Michael chuckles.

"Roni, that's enough cheese! You know you're going to get the shits after."

"No! Keep going!" She laughs.

Michael twirls away and leaves after serving us our entrées.

Steam emerges from Veronica's chicken parmesan. It looks nothing like the picture from the promotional menu. The chicken is smaller, there are only five pieces of broccoli, and the dried up marinara sauce hugs only half of the breaded chicken.

Veronica picks at the cheese with her fork and takes a bite. Her eyes roll to the back of her head.

"Mmm, fuck that's so good," she moans.

"Really? Can I have a bite?" I reach my fork over to her plate.

"Hell nah," she laughs, swatting away my hand.

"So, what did you say when you found out?"

"You should've seen my face when they called me back. I literally yelled, 'You're joking,' when they told me. I couldn't believe it. But I don't have it anymore. It was treated so easily."

"Did you see any symptoms?"

"No! That's the thing, I barely had any symptoms. But the doctor told me that happens sometimes."

"Well... at least you're okay now. Can you like, please be careful next time, though?" I sigh. I stab a sun-dried tomato, bowtie pasta, and a mushroom on one bite.

"Yeah, yeah, I know," she replies.

"I don't know man. I know you get caught up in the moment and shit, but just protect yourself, alright? Ask your dudes if they've been tested or something."

"Yeah, girl... but since I'm on the pill it's so much easier not to use a condom." She shrugs. "I know, I know, it's dumb of me, but don't worry man, next time I will for sure."

Michael skips to our table. "How are you guys doing? Is the food good?"

We both smile and nod.

"It's so freakin' good, thanks!" Veronica responds.

"Okay, great! Need more cheese girlie? Ha!"

Michael winks and twirls away.

"You know what the fucked-up part is?" Veronica asks.

"What?"

"Well, I don't really care if I get it again because I can just take pills and it will go away anyways."

"What the fuck, Roni?"

"Yeah… I know," she chuckles. "But seriously, I just had to take pills for a week and it went away."

"Shake my head, Roni. Don't fuck around like that."

"Yeah, yeah. Don't worry, I'm going to be careful now."

I look across the table at her plate. Veronica is more than halfway done her pile of cheese and chicken parmesan. I look over to my plate and notice that I've taken only a few bites.

"So, how's your family doing, by the way?" Veronica asks.

For the rest of the night, I didn't eat my pasta. I ask Michael to pack the rest of my food to go. I drop Veronica to her house and I drive the rest of the way home in silence. When I get to my bedroom, I slouch in my twin-sized bed, wrap myself in my cotton blanket and I look at my phone.

Veronica texts me.

Erika, man. You were right, I shouldn't have eaten all that cheese. I have diarrhea now.

I *told you so.* I reply.

someone once told me that my handwriting is ugly

now this book is filled with it

perception is a great thing

baby shower

I sit on the wooden pew at Merciful Redeemer Church. My eyes are heavy. Father Dave's voice weaves slowly in and out of my head. My eyes shut. My body shakes and I snort myself awake. Father Dave rambles about how the birth of a child is a wonderful gift, the birth of Jesus is a miracle, and the birth of his annoying nephew is a nightmare. The rows of Catholics chuckle deeply to Father Dave's joke.

After church, my mom, dad, and sister Haley hop in our green Suzuki.

"Where do you want to eat? Wendy's?" my dad asks as he flicks on his left signal to turn on Eglinton Avenue West.

Haley and I both look at each other and smirk.

"Yes, dad," says Haley.

Every Sunday after church we go to the Wendy's and Tim Horton's beside Erin Mills Town Centre. Instead of eating inside today, we decide to get take out. We wait behind five other cars in the drive thru. Five minutes later, my mom whispers to my dad in a loud voice.

"Ay, Daddy, we should tell Erika and Haley yung sino buntis."

I look at Haley and roll my eyes.

"I can hear you mom. What are you talking about?"

"Ay, uhhh... Anak," my mom mumbles. "Your Tita Neta call me, she invite us to Ate Mia's baby shower. She's buntis with Kuya Richard's baby."

Haley swipes her head left and stares at me with her eyes widened. I mirror the same look.

"W-w-what?" I say.

My mom and Tita Neta used to work together at an electronic company where they tested microwaves. While growing up, Ate Mia would come over to our apartment and Haley, her, and I played hand games and with our new Barbies.

One day, we decided to make up a game and pretend that we were animals in the zoo. The three of us sat under the wooden table in the middle of the kitchen. Ate Mia went on all fours and growled as she crawled closer to me.

"I'm a lion, I'm going to eat you!"

I crawled as fast as I could around the table's legs. My knees scraped across the white marble of the kitchen floor as her shadow chased me around the wooden poles. This was one of my last memories of Ate Mia, four years ago.

In March, Ate Mia's parents threw a surprise baby shower at River Grove Community Centre near Creditview Road and Britannia. Haley and I sit beside each other at a table with our parents. My mom's sister, Tita Myla, and my grandparents sit with us too. They came an hour early to help Tita Neta set up for the party. Tita Neta approaches Haley and I with Styrofoam plates and plastic utensils, and motions us to the buffet table.

"Kain na tayo! There's so much food."

"Thanks Tita!" I look over at the two long tables filled with Filipino food. At least ten bowls and trays with pancit, Lechon, Adobo, spring rolls, and rice. At the end of the table is the dessert: sticky rice cake wrapped in banana leaves, and five flan cakes.

"This is weird," I say to Haley while scooping a spoon of white rice. "I can't believe Ate Mia is pregnant."

"I know, she's only sixteen… that's like us in five years," Haley says.

"I think the strangest part is that Ate Mia could've been with anyone but... she's with Kuya Richard... such a coincidence," I say.

Haley and I grew up with Kuya Richard too. Whoever's birthday it was, Kuya Richard's parents or my parents would host parties at their house. We called these gatherings "famjams." At every one of these functions, we would stay up until 1:00 a.m. with Kuya Richard's brother, JR, and their cousin, Neal. We stayed up playing Monopoly or an exciting game of truth or dare.

"Yeah, it's strange because they've never met each other at a famjam," Haley says.

"I think they met through Neal or something," I say.

After waiting thirty minutes for Ate Mia and Kuya Richard to come, Tita Neta hushed at the crowd.

"Be quiet everyone! They're coming!"

The crowd of thirty Titos and Titas hush for a few moments. The grey doors creak open.

Everyone yells, "SURPRISE!"

The booming sound is accompanied with hard claps and whistles.

Ate Mia stares at the crowd of Filipinos and doesn't flinch at the room full of cheers. She doesn't smile. She doesn't say a word. Kuya Richard, standing to her right, has a wide grin. He raises his hand to thank everyone. Tita Neta leads Ate Mia and Kuya Richard to a long rectangular table at the front of the party room. The two of them sit at the head table like a husband and wife would at their wedding. Ate Mia's face is still blank.

For the rest of the party, Ate Mia's head hangs low. She doesn't speak to anyone for the rest of the afternoon. Before leaving, Tita Neta hands a microphone to Kuya Richard to say thanks.

"Hi, everyone. I just want to say thank you from the both of us, to all of you for coming. We really appreciate the love and support." He waves and nods.

After the baby shower, my family and I get in our car and head to Tim Hortons for tea and hot chocolate. During the car ride, my mom's voice trembles.

"Daddy, I think she is ashamed, ha?" she says in broken English.

"Well, yeah… she only sixteen. She's still in school." He breathes heavily. "Erika, Haley, you both finish school. Boys can wait, okay?" he says.

"Yes, daddy," we say together.

I look outside my window and think about Ate Mia having to change a baby's diaper, having to feed her baby, and giving birth at the hospital. I think about the time when Ate Mia took care of Haley and me. We went to her house while our parents went to the Casino.

"Ate Mia, I'm hungry," Haley said.

There was no food to eat at her house. The last time we ate was at lunch, but now it was two hours past dinner.

"Okay, don't worry," she smiled. "I can make you some food. I just learned how to cook eggs."

"Wow, you know how to cook eggs?" I said.

"Well it's not that hard. I'll show you guys."

Ate Mia took out a large, black pan, and placed it on top of the white stove. She turned the dial to maximum heat, grabbed oil from under the cupboard, poured it into the pan, and waited for it to heat. She took out a brown carton from the fridge and plucked out a few eggs.

"So, first you heat up the oil, and then you crack your eggs over the pan."

She broke the eggs over the crackling oil, mixing the egg whites and yolk together with a rubber spatula.

"Wooow! That's so cool!" I said. "I can't wait until I learn how to cook."

"You're a grown up now, huh, Ate Mia?" Haley said.

We watched the eggs turn into a fluffy texture. She scraped

the dried egg around the edges of the pan with the spatula. She turned off the heat and opened her cupboard, grabbing salt and pepper to season.

"Tada!" said Ate Mia, "There are your eggs!" She raises both hands in the air and praises the fried eggs. She tippy toed to the top of the cabinet, reached for three plates, scooped rice, and placed it on one side of the plate, leaving room on the other side for the eggs.

"Wow, I've only ever seen my dad cook eggs before," I said.

"Yeah, Ate Mia. Only parents know how to cook! You would make a great mom!" said Haley.

Ate Mia laughed. "Yeah, that's gonna be like a million years from now."

pregnant at starbucks

❀

Sam and I sit in our fourth period class, *Introduction to Accounting*, with Mrs. Beam. She finished teaching us how to balance an income statement sheet and gave us the remainder of class to do our homework.

Sam and I met in Grade 6. Throughout high school, we spent lunch together eating Chinese food at Mr. Dumpling or hanging out after school at the park to drink vodka out of our flasks. Last year, we graduated from high school. This year we both decided to stay back for a victory lap to upgrade our marks and to take courses that we needed for college and university.

We sit on the left side of the classroom, in the back row

next to the bookshelves of extra accounting textbooks. Every day in class, we whisper different sex stories instead of doing our assigned homework. Today, she tells me a story about her friend Joanne.

"So, Joanne and this guy were just making out and shit, right?" She presses her thick lips together, holding in a laugh.

"Then, they go to second base, so like, she takes off her top and then…" Sam continues.

"Shhh!" Mrs. Beam glares at us. "Please stop talking you two, people are trying to do work."

Sam lowers her voice. "Then… he just came on her randomly."

"Wait… what the fuck?" I giggle. "They didn't even have sex?"

"No!" Sam laughs. "I guess he was just so turned on."

"What the hell? God, that's a messed-up story."

"Yeah, I know, right?" Sam wipes away her tears. "So, how are you and Mark doing?"

"We're doing really good. We hang every weekend. The only thing is that…"

"Girls! Please be quiet!" says Mrs. Beam.

Sam rolls her eyes.

I lower my voice. "I missed my period..." I whisper. "I was supposed to get it like five days ago."

"Oh shit, eh? Don't worry you're probably not prego," Sam says. "Did you do a pregnancy test?"

"No... I'm too scared to check. Will you buy one with me after school?"

"Hell yeah, girl. We'll go to Metro after class."

After school, Sam and I hop off the Milton transit at the Milton Go bus stop. We cross the street to the Metro on Thompson.

"Fuck, I really hope I'm not pregnant. My parents will seriously kill me."

"Shit... did you tell Mark already?"

"Nah, not yet. I want to make sure before saying anything."

"Yeah that's true. Don't need a pregnancy scare for nothin'. What would he do if he found out you were pregnant?"

"Sam... I don't even wanna think about that now. We're not ready for kids... and I don't want to think about aborting our first kid."

We walk down the hallway, reading the aisle signs: *condiments, bread, Asian, and Pads and Birth Planning*. I slowly stride down the Birth Planning aisle. I scan through the items on the shelf. The top row for lube, then condoms. I find the pregnancy sticks by the Vagisil feminine wash and Advil. I look at the three-different pregnancy stick brands and bite on my bottom lip.

"Bro, which do I get? These all look the damn same," I say.

"Don't kill me… I know. It's so confusing. Just get this one." Sam points to a bright pink box labelled with the eye-rolling statement, "Six days sooner than your missed period."

I pick up the *First Response Pregnancy Test* and double-check the price.

"Sam… you think you could cash this out for me, please? Sara's working today and I don't want her to see me with this…"

"Yeah girl, just pass me your card on check out."

Sam and I walk to the self-checkout and cash out the box.

"Yo, wanna go to Starbucks after this? I wanna try their new Frappuccino. Plus, I got a gift card from some guy I'm seeing."

"Yeah, I'm down. I think I'll do the test in the single stall washroom there."

We walk down the street to the Starbucks beside Metro. Sam's long brown hair shines in the light. We go inside the dim coffee shop and a waft of espresso hits me.

"I'm gonna order my drink. I'll meet you in the washroom. You want anything?"

"I'm good, thanks."

She stands in line waiting behind a lanky, bald man with strong Axe cologne and a faux leather jacket. I lay my head low, walk past the espresso bar, and head straight to the back of the store.

I knock on the wooden door, turn the cold metal handle and walk in. I pull out a long strip of toilet paper, fold it in half, and place it on the toilet seat. After I finish my makeshift toilet seat cover, I read the instructions on the box.

Sam walks in the washroom.

"Hey, did you do it yet?"

"Uh… not yet… Just about to." My hand shakes as I hold the box in my hand.

The room smells like urine. Bits of toilet paper are scattered across the bathroom floor, and small flies hover near the toilet.

I pull down my black leggings, strip my pink underwear, and sit on the toilet.

"Here," Sam rips open the pregnancy box and pulls out one of the sticks.

"You're supposed to pee on this and then we'll wait to see

if the stick turns pink or blue or something," she says while sipping on her grande salted caramel Frappuccino.

A bead of sweat drips down my temple.

"Fuck. Thanks, Sam. I'm really scared. I don't wanna be a damn mom… "

My hand trembles reaching for the wrapped pee stick in her hand.

"Honestly, I really doubt you're pregnant. You use protection, right? So, don't worry about it." Sam smiles, her right dimple peeking through her cheek. She rubs my left shoulder.

I rip open the package and place the tip of the pregnancy stick under me. I stare at the floor as my pee trickles on the stick. I take a deep breath before removing the test.

I look down. The stick isn't pink or blue.

It's red.

"What the fuck. Sam, I just got my period. I just bled all over the stick."

"Oh my God. Ew! That's disgusting," Sam laughs.

She falls to the floor and continues cackling. I laugh harder. She wipes her tears away and takes a sip of her grande salted caramel crème Frapp.

self-love

it took me a long time to love myself
& i am not even fully there

loving bits of yourself that you've hated for so long is
tough
overwhelming
difficult

so, why is it so hard to love ourselves?

i mean it doesn't have to be hard, of course, but everyone
is always searching to love ourselves more and more

and why is it never *why don't i hate myself?*

shower hands ♡

I stand in the shower. Warm water drips slowly down my neck. The steam from the shower trails across the metal rod of the shower curtain. The grease from my scalp mixes with the water. I run my fingers along my hair and massage my head.

I've been standing in this shower for twenty minutes. I haven't touched my Head and Shoulders lavender shampoo, or reached for my pink loofah. Instead, I stare at my warm, tan skin, absorbing the water droplets.

The shower water blends with my tears as it hits my face. I differentiate the liquid with salty drops trailing the edge of my bottom lip.

Fuck, I hate myself so much.

Earlier this year, I moved to Mississauga and started my last year at high school at St. Joes.

I replay my Philosophy teacher, Mr. Gordon, asking if I have any friends to borrow notes from.

I told him no.

Why did he have to call me out like that? So fucking awkward.

"Well you need to get some friends," he told me.

For the past few days, I spent lunch standing in different washroom stalls to pass the time. No one would eat lunch with me.

I think about how it feels to have no friends at school.

Just kill yourself already, no one will care anyways.

I run my fingers through my wet skin. I think about jumping off the balcony in the family room. I open the balcony door, feel the cool fall breeze, grip the thin metal railing, and push off. The rust grazes my fingers.

It's only a few meters down though. That won't do much damage.

I picture myself jumping off the balcony. My bones breaking as I hit the pavement.

But it's only a few meters…. Would I even die? Fuck, I don't want to try to kill myself and still live…

I shake my head side to side. Water from my black, tangled hair splashes across the floral shower curtain to my right and along the ceramic tiles to my left.

I try to ignore the thoughts, but they are stronger today.

No one fucking cares about you.

I curl my toes.

You're stupid, you're ugly, and you have no friends.

I scrunch my eyes and blink away the water and tear mixture. I cross my arms along my chest and focus on the puddle forming in the crevice of my arms, inside of my elbows.

I look down at my stomach. My gold belly ring is dulled from six years of clinging to my navel. I grab the bulge of my belly and wiggle the piece of skin.

Fuck, I'm so fat. I need to lose some damn weight.

I make a fist and punch myself in the belly. Gently.

My eyes glaze over my metal shower caddy in the corner of my tub. Aussie, three minute miracle moist deep conditioner, half a bottle of Vagisil, my shampoo, and loofa.

I look at the Gillette razor sitting on the middle rack of the caddy. I think about running the blades along my skin and pressing it deeply.

I'm too much of a pussy though. I can't do it.

I sob. My tears blend with the water droplets. It doesn't even feel like I'm crying.

You're so fucking worthless.

I tighten my fist and punch myself again. Harder.

No one cares about you.

The water pressure weighs on my shoulders.

Just kill yourself already.

My fingers dig into my biceps. I look at my untrimmed finger nails. My fingers dig harder on my smooth skin.

I press deeper and drag my nails with as much pressure as I can.

I scratch harder and harder on my biceps.

My raw skin tingles as each drop of warm water hits my arms.

Fuck, I don't want anyone to see these scratches.

I press my nails on my chest and leave trails above my breasts instead. I dig my nails deep and leave red marks.

Red lines cross and interlock each other, painting paths on my skin. I run my fingers over and over.

You're worthless.

I scrape my nails over and over on my chest.

Eventually, blood mixes with the water.

You don't mean anything to anyone.

My nails dig into my skin transforming it to raw, red lines. Pieces of my skin stick under my nails.

Kill yourself, already.

Someone knocks on the door.

"Anak, I'm going to work na. I love you," my mom says.

I stop digging. I sob. My nose drips.

I place my arms across my chest again and look at my red-stained canvas.

This chest is not mine.

My eyes glance down at my bloody fingernails. I stare at my foreign hands, trembling in the lukewarm water.

More tears flow and join the crevice in my arms. A salty, pink puddle. I reach for the Head and Shoulders and start my shower.

caleb

I walk to the local McDonalds on a rainy and foggy Tuesday evening. Raindrops drip on my glasses. I think about what to order as I walk through the narrow doorway. The cashier greets me.

"Hi. I can help who's next."

"May I please get one junior chicken and one small fries."

"Okay. Is that everything?"

"Yes please. Thanks."

"That will be $9.90. How will you be paying?"

I flash the cashier my debit card and tap it against the card machine. *Beep*. I stare at the back of the kitchen and search for any familiar faces. Since St. Joseph high school was less than a ten-minute drive to the local McDonalds, many students worked there part-time.

My friend Caleb worked at McDonalds, and I couldn't wait for him to greet me. Caleb and I shared senior year together in high school. As a new student, I walked down the long, gray, halls as he accompanied me by putting his arm around my shoulder. He would shine his contagious smile, asked me how I my day was going, and walk away. I would drag myself to my last class, mathematical statistics, but encountering his presence on gloomy days was just enough to push myself through.

I saw Caleb last week as I was passing by the McDonald's drive thru. It was 10:00 p.m. as I rolled by in my gold Pontiac. I saw Caleb's round face dimmed under the pot lights. His face was hidden from the shadow of his McDonald's hat. I waved to him as I passed the first window.

"Hey Caleb, whaddup?"

He squinted at the stranger calling out his name.

"Oh hayyyy, is that Erika? How are ya?" He smiled waving both of his hands in the air. We greeted one another the exact same way every time we saw each other.

"I'm good buddy!" I smiled and waved before driving away.

I search for Caleb through the metal posts of the kitchen

after placing my order. He wore his black uniform with blue stripes down the sleeves of his arms, matching black pants, and a black hat with the crest of the golden "M." His caramel-tone skin compliments the royal blue in his uniform and the warmth in his deep brown eyes. His bright, glowing smile, stretched across his face as he greeted me.

I stop looking behind the metal bars and realize that my friend Caleb isn't there. I take a deep breath and remember. Caleb passed away last week.

He passed away on the week of Halloween. My boyfriend, Mark, called me on the phone to tell me the news. We all went to high school together. I was at the University of Toronto, helping with our student union's haunted house when I got the call.

"Hey…Did you hear what happened to Caleb?" Mark asked.

"What? What do you mean?"

"He passed away…"

The noisy room of students fell silent. My eyes watered. It felt as if I were cutting twenty onions.

"W-what? What happened?"

"He killed himself..." he sniffled. "His parents say it was from depression."

The lady at McDonald's calls out my order.

"One Junior chicken and one small fries. Do you want ketchup with that?"

I walk out of the McDonalds and my mouth waters as the aroma of my burger and French fries create a trail beside me.

I scroll through Facebook and type Caleb's name in the search bar. There are over a hundred posts on his wall with sympathetic thoughts, prayers, and condolences from friends and family.

We will miss your smiling face, RIP.

You won't be forgotten buddy.

I love you Caleb. Rest in peace my handsome brother. I love you so much. We're family forever.

I sniffle. My vision fogs up from my eyes watering. I softly sob to myself while I reach for my earphones in my grey Canada Goose jacket pocket. Tears stroll down my face. I taste the saltiness as it trails near the corners of my mouth. I reach down the brown paper bag and eat a crispy French fry.

angry mama ✿

It's 10:00 p.m. on a chilly Wednesday in November. Mark drives to my house to do our homework together. Whenever he comes over, we debate if we should hang out upstairs in my room or downstairs in the basement. The answer is always the same. I go upstairs while he hangs out in the basement. The basement is cold, there's bugs, and it's cluttered, so I can't focus on my homework. Mark loves to hang down there to watch basketball on the T.V. or play Wii Sports.

Today, my room has piles of laundry on the chair by my desk, dinner receipts from last week, and assignments sprawled across my work area. My carpet is scattered with used socks and Urban Outfitters reusable bags.

"So, you wanna come chill in the basement today or nah?"

"Hm… yeah. I'll go down. My room's a freakin' mess."

His eyes widen. "What? Really?" He smiles.

Mark and I sit on the couch downstairs. He places his MacBook on his lap and edits his client's latest music video. He flips through tabs of rap and hip hop music videos on his laptop, screenshotting scenes for inspiration.

I lay my head on his lap and snuggle my face into his tummy. I wrap my arms around his thick waist, and prop my feet on the couch. I doze off and snore to the clicking of his laptop, and to the sound of the Raptor's basketball game on T.V.

"Lowry passes the ball to DeRozan, makes a quick lay-up and… Ohhh! Another three-pointer by Lowry!"

I wake up to the sound of the garage door creaking. The car engine of my parents' new Honda Civic roars through the basement walls. It's my mom coming home from work. She comes home every night at 11:30 p.m. The engine stops and the garage door closes.

"Hi, Mark!" she yells from the entrance of the garage.

She shuffles her feet across the carpet. Her voice grows louder as she moves closer to the couch.

"How are you, Mark?" she asks.

"Hi, Anak. Do you want me to take those dishes upstairs for you?" she asks me, pointing at the plates on the table with her lips.

My eyes flutter and I slurp the drool from the side of my mouth.

"I'll take it upstairs later," I mumble, my eyes still shut.

"Okay. Who's winning Mark?" My mom asks.

I drool on Mark's thigh. The sounds of the basketball game and my mom's voice mellow in and out.

Four years ago, when Mark and I started dating, we watched our first movie together in my basement. We sat next to each other on the couch. I propped my laptop on the coffee table and plugged in my speakers. It was a movie called *Hard Candy* with Ellen Page and Patrick Wilson. Our fourth period teacher, Miss Riccardi, recommended it to the class last week.

This was the second time that Mark came over to my house. I told my mom that a friend was coming over. She cooked in the kitchen as Mark and I watched the movie in the basement. The aroma of pork Adobo, bay leaves, and rice filled the house.

Half-way through the movie, I placed my head on his lap and wrapped a blanket around my body.

"Wow, this movie sucks," Mark laughed.

I smirked. "Yeah... I thought it would be better since Miss Riccardi suggested it," I said.

I stared at my laptop while Mark ran his fingers through my thick, black hair. I watched Ellen Page drug the guy in the movie, popping pills in his drink.

In the middle of the scene, my mom crept up behind us.

"What are you two doing, ha? Are you boyfriend and girlfriend, ha?" My mom glared at Mark and I on the couch.

"What, mom?" I sat up abruptly. "No, we're not..." I said. My cheeks flushed, my palms dampened.

"You cannot sit like that together, okay?" She pointed at us with her eyebrows furrowed.

I looked over at Mark. My ears felt warm. He nodded and stared at me with blank eyes. I've never seen my mom react this way to my friends or any of our guests. She always welcomed people with "good morning" or "good evening" and asked them how their day was going.

"Mark, I know you are not a bad guy, but I am looking out for Erika." She raised her voice and stammered. "Y-you know, I only have t-two daughters, oookkay?"

Mark nodded.

She was just in the kitchen... did she come down the basement to on creep us? Was she spying on us this whole time?

"Okay, I will not tolerate this! You cannot act this way in my house!" My mom yelled and stomped out of the basement, leaving footprints on the carpet. She stomped up the stairs and walked back to the kitchen.

"Oh my God... I'm so sorry," I apologized.

I didn't look up. I couldn't look at his face.

Mark laughed. "Don't worry about it. I get it."

Mark gently shakes my shoulders, kisses my forehead, and wakes me up from my nap.

"Ew, you drooled on my jeans," he whines.

I open my eyes and yawn.

"Oops," I laugh, wiping the side of my face.

"Okay, I'm heading home now. It's getting late."

We bring the dishes to the kitchen and walk to the foyer. I wait for Mark to tie his shoes.

"Babe, remember when my mom yelled at you that time we watched that dumb movie?" I laugh. "It's crazy that that was four years ago..."

Mark laughs. The lines around his eyes wrinkle.

"Wow, that's insane. I can't believe it's been that long."

"Yeah, thought you would've left my annoying ass by

now."

"Shut up, stupid." He laughs, punching my right shoulder.

"Ow! What the fuck, that hurt."

"You're such a liar. Oh my God, I barely touched you."

We hear footsteps shuffle to the top of the steps. We look up at the stairs leading from the foyer to the kitchen. My mom hovers above and looks down at us. She wears a tattered grey t-shirt and long baggy shorts. Her toes peek out of her floral slippers.

"Mark, you leaving na?"

"Yes, Tita! Bye, goodnight." Mark waves.

"Ah, okay. Drive safe!" she smiles, squinting her eyes. "See you tomorrow, ha." She shuffles back to the kitchen.

paul ♂

Last year for Halloween, I painted my face blue with eyeshadow. Shades of sky blue highlighted my forehead, chin, and nose. Deep indigo contoured my plump cheeks and structured my double-chin. I slipped into a grey, wool turtleneck that I bought from Value Village. I dressed up as Sadness from *Inside Out*. My outfit was perfect. The only thing missing was Sadness' short blue bob cut. I found a short blond wig and spray painted it with blue hair dye for an hour in my garage.

My friend, Anthony, from high school threw a Halloween party at his house for the first time. He invited a few friends from school and promised pizza and booze. Before leaving the house, I looked at my Sadness costume in the mirror to double check that my outfit was complete. I drew on thick, black slanted eyebrows on my face, put on my oversized glasses, and smiled at myself in the mirror. My face spoke otherwise.

I arrived at the party at 10:30 p.m. Anthony greeted me at the door. He guided me down the stairs to his basement. The loud bass and smell of vodka filtered the air. I walked down the stairs and found my friends, Angelica and Danielle, already drinking on the couch. Angelica had a bottle of Budweiser in her hand and Danielle had a cocktail of rum and coke — our favourite.

"Sup y'all!" I said.

"Yooooo… Erika," Danielle slurred. "I missed you man. I'm drunk," she laughed.

Angelica waved to me and sipped her beer. I hugged them both. Next to them sat Paul. We all went to the same high school, Bishop Reding. I sat with them on the couch.

"Hey Erika, what's up?" Paul said.

"Holy shit, I haven't seen you in forever. How've you been?"

I met Paul in Mrs. Lehtoverra's Grade 5 class. We sat in the same row. When he laughed, his blond hair bounced like wind was passing it. My classmates, Angelica, Anthony, and I would pretend to have our own talk show. His bright laugh echoed off the metal walls of the portable.

He talked to me about his new job and how he went to Sheridan for school.

This was the last memory I had of Paul.

A year later, on October 20th, Paul passed away. I found out while scrolling through my Facebook timeline four days after his passing. I scrolled through my feed and came across a post a friend from high school shared.

The most beautiful flowers get picked first. Rest in peace, Paul.

My fingers twitch as I click on Paul's profile page. Paul and I weren't close, but I couldn't breathe knowing he was gone. I scroll through his timeline. Friends and classmates from high school share their memories of him. I rub my dry eyes. I browse each message on his wall.

They all shared the link to his tribute page from the J. Scott Early Funeral Homes website. A square picture of a marigold flower with violet daisies are next to the text "Obituary of Paul."

His obituary reads: "Paul was a kind and humble young man who touched so many lives with his compassionate personality, sunshine in his eyes, and the warmest smile."

Two days later, I pick up Angelica on the way to Paul's memorial service in Milton. It's Wednesday, October 26th. The black sky matches the asphalt from the heavy rain. We drive downtown Milton searching for the funeral home.

"Do you know where it is?" I ask.

"Yeah, I've passed by it a few times when I'm downtown Milton," she says, flipping her golden hair behind her ear.

We drive by the building. Red brick, white pane windows with black shutters. Each window is lit with fluorescent light. Groups of people surround the entrance. Angelica and I find a parking spot behind the building, in front of the Milton Denture Clinic.

"Fuck I'm scared. I don't want to go inside," Angelica's voice shakes.

"I know me too…" I sigh. "I'm so glad we're going to this together though."

"Yeah same. This is so fucked up."

"I wonder what happened to him…" I say.

Angelica stares at me with bloodshot eyes. "You don't know? They found him… hanging…"

We walk to the funeral home. A few of Paul's mourners stand near the bare oak tree down the street. The tree staggers over three figures in front of it. Their shadows from the street light casts a dim glow on their faces. It's Jash, Sami, and Bryan. Paul's best friends. One of them holds a lit cigarette in their left hand. Angelica grips my wrist as we pass the doors of the building. There's a line-up of people leading into a room with Paul's family and his casket. We stand in the back of the line, surpassing the doors. I look around to see if I recognize anyone. I stand beside Angelica, waiting to say our condolences to his family.

I rub my hands along my black jeans to wipe off the sweat. I couldn't help but think of what Angelica said to me in the car. I didn't know Paul was depressed. I didn't know that he was going through things at home. I didn't know he took his own life.

We inch closer into the room.

I stare at my feet as I shuffle across the carpet.

Angelica nudges me and points to a book held up on an easel. It's Paul's guest book of all the condolences, flowers, and candles that were lit on his tribute page online.

My condolences to the family. Great memories of him from high school.

Paul was a kind soul and will be sadly missed.

We shuffle closer. We're five people away from shaking his parent's hands.

I watch the pattern of the people in front of me. They shake Paul's dad's hand, apologize for his loss, and do the same thing to Paul's mom, then Paul's brother. They follow the line towards Paul's casket and sit to pray or walk into another room.

Angelica stands in front of me. I'm next in line to shake their hands.

She follows the pattern.

My head lays low.

Why did Paul take his own life? Did he tell anyone?

My arms are numb.

I wish I could've done more for him.

My eyes water, my fingers tremble.

Instead of reaching my hand out to Paul's family, I cover my face and sob. I wipe my tears and bow my head, passing each family member. I couldn't look at them.

I grab Angelica's hand as she waits for me at the end of the line. Her hand is clammy. We walk together to Paul's casket and sit on the maroon, cushioned chairs in the front of the room and pray.

My breath shakes as I mouth the Hail Mary. I look up and see Paul's Facebook photo. He's standing in the middle of an empty street, the sun glistens against his blonde hair, and the yellow buildings cascade over him.

The photo is in a gold frame propped on an easel like his guest book in the back of the room. His closed casket shines under the spotlights. I close off my prayer to say a few personal words for Paul.

I know that we weren't best friends or even great friends. But we were friends, and I wish I was there for you when you needed someone. May you rest peacefully now, Paul. We are all thinking about you.

I whisper under my breath a tweet that I saw on Paul's profile a few hours ago before coming to the viewing.

I can already tell today is going to be a good day.

I dry my cheeks and motion my fingers in the sign of the cross.

Amen.

pink flower

On Thursday, I walk into UTM's Health Counselling Centre. There's no line up today. I stand in front of the sign that says, "Please respect other students' privacy and wait for your turn to be called up." I wait for the lady behind the front desk to call my name.

"Next!" she calls out in a shrill voice.

"Hi, I'm here for a 3:00 p.m. appointment with Dr. Simons."

I hand her my health card and University of Toronto student card.

"Thanks, Erika. Please have a seat. They'll call your name shortly."

The waiting area is sectioned off with gray chairs, facing outward, placed in the shape of a "U." In the center of the chairs is a cream-coloured, four-legged table. On the table are eight mini clipboards with black-and-white printed photos of abstract flowers and vines, and a black UTM mug with different coloured pencil crayons. I pick up a pink pencil, colour in the petals of a tulip and wait for Dr. Simons.

I wait to get my first pap smear done.

A few days earlier, I asked my friend Veronica what her first pap smear was like.

"I mean… I can see why they recommend you to take it when you're not a virgin." Sam laughs. "It hurts like a bitch."

"Oh damn, what do you mean?"

"I can't imagine what it would be like if you never had sex before and felt that shit. They pretty much shove something in you and open up your vagina."

"Oh shit, eh… I just scheduled my pap smear with my doctor at UTM."

"Don't worry, you'll be fine. It goes by fast. It's just in out and then it's over."

Ten minutes later, a blond nurse calls my name. Dropping my pencil crayon, I look up from my pink masterpiece and place the mini clipboard back on the square table and follow the nurse. I walk past room #1 and #2, and make my way to the last room down the hall. Dr. Simons sits in front of her medical computer next to a green patient's chair. I've been seeing Dr. Simons for the past eight months to renew my birth control prescription. During my last visit, she told me that since I'm twenty-one, it's recommended I get my pap smear done.

"Hi, Erika. Welcome back," says Dr. Simons as she adjusts her silver rectangular frames.

"Hey, Dr. Simons. How are you?"

"I'm well. So, it's your first pap smear today?"

"Yes."

"That's great, let's get started. I'm going to examine your abdomen first before proceeding with your pap smear," she says.

I nod.

"Okay Erika, let's get you on the blue bed and I'll get you to please lie down on your back."

I lie down on the crinkly wax paper that runs down the middle of the stiff blue bed. I breathe deeply and exhale through my mouth. Dr. Simons lifts my grey sweater over my belly button and applies pressure on my lower abdomen.

"Does this hurt?" she asks, pressing firmly on my left side.

I grip the sides of the bed tight with my fingers, crumpling the paper.

"No," I squeak.

Dr. Simon's index and middle finger press down on my right side, over my ovaries. My eyes bounce from staring at the ceiling and back to her face. She bites her lip as she presses down hard and rubs the area.

"Does this hurt?"

I feel her nails digging into my side.

I respond again. "No."

"So, I'm going to ask you to remove your bottoms now. I'm sorry that we don't have a curtain for you to change behind, but I'm just going to turn around and you can tell me when you're ready."

"Oh, o-okay," I stutter.

I unbutton my pants and slowly slide down my black jeans to my ankles. I forgot that I put on my pink long johns today. They slide down with my pants and tickle my leg hairs. I slide down my cotton underwear, and leave them hanging down my ankles with my long johns and jeans.

"Um, Dr. Simons do you want me to take off my pants completely… or… uh, is it okay if I leave them around my ankles?"

"Please remove them completely."

The cool breeze from the fan above me blows through the hair on my arms. Bumps form on my skin. I lay my back on the stiff bed. My back glides against the smooth wax paper. I prop my feet on the table and bend me knees as if I'm ready to do some crunches.

"Okay, Dr. Simons. I'm ready."

I keep the rest of my clothes on. I fiddle with the ends of my grey sweater as I wait for Dr. Simons to turn around.

Oh, God. It's okay if she sees your vagina… She's a doctor, Erika. Don't be nervous.

Dr. Simons turns around and looks at my position.

"Oh my, you look uncomfortable," she laughs.

She walks over and stands in front me.

"You need to move your bottom closer to your ankles for me, they're too far from each other. I need you to slide your back down."

Dr. Simons places her hands on my shoulders and slides me down. The paper rubs against my butt.

"Okay, there you go," she says.

My butt cheeks touch my ankles.

Dr. Simons moves in front of my vagina. I bend my neck

and look down to see her face in between my legs. I watch as she snaps on blue latex gloves. She prepares the tools for the procedure and I hear the metal torture devices clank together on the silver tray.

I look away and focus my eyes on the patterns on the ceiling instead. I stare at the grey spots.

16x16, off-white tiles, dark grey specs cover the square. How many tiles are on this ceiling? I wonder if the other rooms have the same ceiling tiles.

"Do you know what happens during the procedure?" she asks while holding up a thick, metal clamp. The device looks like a combination of chicken wing tongs and a dildo.

I shake my head. "No. I don't."

"Well, I insert the tip," she points to the round phallic tip of the clamp, "and I slide it inside your vagina." She motions the clamp in the air.

"Then I open the clamp inside to open your cervix so I can see if there are any abnormalities," she says as she opens the clamp by pressing a metal tab attached to the handle.

My eyes widen.

What the fuck is that thing? She's going to put that metal shit in my vagina?

"Once the clamp is open, I will take this swab," Dr.

Simons shows me the long white swab that looks like the longest Q-tip I've ever seen. At the end of the Q-tip is a blue comb with prickly edges sticking out.

"Then, I will put it in and swab the inside of your cervix to collect the tissue cells inside," she continues.

I can feel the heat and moisture in my armpits, but I feel the cool air-conditioning tingling my bare legs and vagina.

"After, I will put this swab in a clear tube that has a liquid substance to preserve the cells until we bring it to the lab for testing. And that's it!" Dr. Simons smiles. The lines around her eyes wrinkle.

I blink rapidly.

"Oh… okay," I say as my fingers grip tighter on the side of the bed.

Dr. Simons stands in front of my vagina and grabs a tube of lube and rubs it on the tip of the chicken-wing-dildo device.

I look up at the ceiling.

16×16… off-white… light spots.

She inserts the tip. I feel a sharp pain. The cold metal is slowly pushed further into my vagina. The clamp opens. A draft enters.

Holy fuck, what is happening.

Dr. Simons takes the long Q-tip brush, swabs my cervix,

and removes the clamp in one quick motion.

I finally let out a deep exhale. My heart pounds unevenly.

"Okay, Erika. Now that part one is over," I look down in between my legs and watch Dr. Simons put more lube on the tip of her finger, "I just need to feel the inside of your vagina for any other internal abnormalities."

Oh, my God. What? It's not over? She's gonna finger me now?

Dr. Simons flashes me a reassuring smile. "Don't worry hun, everything looks fine. You're almost done."

"Okay, Dr. Simons. No problem."

I inhale and imagine myself sitting in the waiting room, colouring the pink tulips.

i looked back at some of my old tweets
& realized that i tweeted the same thing every few
years

& that was to tell the people that you love, you love
them

strange that i thought about this so often

but i do love you

sober sophia ✿

For the past two years, on the week of Halloween, a friend of mine has passed away. This year, on October 18th, my friend Sophia overdosed on crack. Thankfully, she didn't die. She just came back from a wedding in the Dominican a few days before.

Sophia texted me:

I'm in the hospital.

What? Why? Are you okay?

Kinda :(I overdosed :(Wake up call I guess...

Sophia has been smoking crack for a year. At first, she only smoked weed and drank alcohol, but when she started hanging out with her boyfriend, Big Daddy. He introduced her to cocaine and crack. She met Big Daddy at Starbucks, near Erin Mills, where she works. He came to Starbucks every day to talk to her, then he started taking her out on dates. Big Daddy sold drugs.

Six months ago, Sophia found out Big Daddy's real name. She searched his name on Google and found out that he's a convicted member for Milton's prostitution ring in 2011, near one of the high schools. She said she would stop talking to him after that.

The next day I went to Credit Valley Hospital with Melanie. Sophia, Melanie, and I are best friends. You would find the three of us together during lunch at school and after school at the local Superstore getting frozen pizza. Mel picked me up at 7:30 p.m. after class in her grey Honda Civic. I haven't seen her in over a month.

"Fuck, I can't believe Soph is in here," Mel says.

"I know… me neither," I say. "She told me she was doing well and stopped smoking for a month. But I guess when she came back from the Dominican she missed it, and took it again…"

Mel parks in the Erin Mills parking lot across the hospital. We walk across the street in our fall coats and thick scarves. The wind blows in Mel's tangled hair.

Inside the hospital, we hop in the elevator to the second floor and find room 1C. Before going inside Soph's room, the nurse tells us that it's required to put on disposable yellow scrubs and wear blue latex gloves. I take off my jacket and pull my arms through the thin, rough yellow fabric, and snap on a pair of gloves.

"Bro, we look like we're from *Breaking Bad*, ready to cook some meth," Mel laughs.

We walk in Soph's room. It's a white room with a thick cream-coloured curtain wrapping around her bed. A washroom is on the right, with her leftover lunch of Shepherd's Pie and a cup of diced peaches on a tray. Her food is untouched. On one side of her bed is a worn-out wooden cabinet and the other side, a matching bedside drawer. Two chairs for Mel and me are at the foot of the bed. The room smells like Lysol disinfectant and boiled eggs.

"Hi guys! I'm happy to see you!" Soph says.

Soph's skin is glowing, her lips are pink and plump, and she hasn't lost any weight.

"We're happy to see you too," Mel says.

I reach over to hug Soph. She puts both palms out in front of her.

"Sorry, I can't hug you guys. They said I might be contagious," Soph said.

The doctors never confirmed why Sophia might be contagious. I guess that it was because she got really sick after being on so much crack.

Mel and I air hug her instead.

"How are you feeling, Soph?" I ask.

Her faded blue hospital gown gently wraps around her figure. Her wet, uncombed hair drapes down to her waist, and her round eyes sink in her deepened eye bags.

"I'm okay. I tried eating, but I keep throwing up."

Two hours pass by. The three of us explore the hospital and talk, so Soph can get her daily exercise. We talk about high school and gossip about people we graduated with having babies and getting engaged.

We walk up the stairs. Mel stands in front of Soph while I'm behind her. Step after step, she puts one foot after another. She can't walk up without resting and panting. Ten minutes go by as Mel and I wait for Soph to reach the top of the stairs.

"Holy shit. I'm tired. This diaper is rubbing up my ass," she says.

We talk about our sleepovers. Soph and I would grab McD's and watch an episode from *That 70's Show*, where Eric, Dona, Hyde, and Kelso would sit in the stoner's circle.

We talk about the last time the three of us hung out. We

shotgunned a few Molson's and played a game of pin the horn on the unicorn, that we found from Dollarama.

After the stroll, we take Sophia back to her room, put on another pair of paper thin scrubs and blue latex gloves, and sit inside. She shows us gifts that Big Daddy got her. Three pairs of jeans embellished with blue flowers in three different sizes, because her weight fluctuates, a big blue fluffy teddy bear, and two pairs of slippers that say "Canada" on the front in pink and red.

"Bro, why the fuck did he buy these ugly ass pants for you?" Mel laughs.

"I know right! I told him that he should've just gave me money, but he knows I'm going to spend it on drugs," she admits.

I look over at Mel. She nods her head and plays with the ripped holes that she made in her yellow scrubs. I look back at Sophia sipping on her Styrofoam cup of water.

"Guys, when I get out of here I'm going to change my life. I'm going to eat healthy and stop doing drugs."

She looks up at us with her tired hazel eyes and smiles.

"I promise. I'm going to change."

shut up old john

It's a cool July afternoon in Mississauga. I stand in the doorway in the middle of the barista station in Second Cup, near Mavis and Eglinton. It leads to the back room where our lids, syrup mixtures, and snacks hide. The black and white analog clock sits above the doorway with the red hand close to 12:00 p.m. There are only four more hours until my shift ends.

I walk to the coffee grinders and shuffle a silver bag of Second Cup's Belgian Chocolate coffee beans and pour them in a round white filter. I tip the beans from the filter and watch them trickle down the dusty grinder machine. I check the dial to make sure it's on grind number seven, and flip the switch. *Grrrrrr.*

The aroma of coconut and chocolate swirls around the station.

It's my second week working at this location. I usually work at Second Cup in Square One, but my boss, Jim, asked if I could help at Mavis because he's short-staffed. Whenever Jim asks for a favour like working at Mavis for just one day, and you say yes, he will schedule you for the next month without asking again. I don't mind, but I would rather be cleaning toilets at Square One.

A customer saunters through the door. It's John. Not Young John, who is 25-years-old, orders a large green tea double-cupped, and plays online poker for a living, but Old John. Old John is a 60-year-old man who orders medium coffees and attends Sheridan College studying human resources.

He wears a beige and olive-striped dress shirt with khaki pants and brown dress shoes. His grey comb over frames his oval-shaped head, matching the thick grey and white speckled moustache living on his face. I glide over to the coffee station and pour his regular order, a medium dark roast with three ice cubes. The deep, rich, bitter fragrance follows me as I walk over to the cash register.

"Hey, John," I say. "How are you?"

"I'm good. How are you, uh…" John taps his long,

wrinkled finger on his head, and curls his lip. "Oh... I can't remember your name. What is it again?"

I stride behind the cash register, place the medium coffee in front of John and smile.

"It's Erika."

John scans his points card in front of the black machine next to the cash register. A laser beam flashes on the plastic card. He hands me a five-dollar bill.

"Thanks John. Your change is two dollars and thirty cents."

John visits the café every day at 4:00 p.m. He drinks his coffee and reads the Toronto Sun by the corner fireplace for a few hours. This is my tenth time serving John this week.

My co-worker, Mariana, warns me that John can blabber for hours, even if there's a line of annoyed customers forming behind him. Mariana has worked for Jim for the past four years.

Today, Mariana opened the store at 7:00 a.m. and served our regulars: Todd, the pale and buff single Americano guy who comes in five times a day. Mia Martina, a Canadian artist from Metal Works, a music production studio behind Mavis. She orders an extra sweet vanilla bean latte with soy milk and light foam every day.

Mariana told me that Old John came into the store last week and told her she's a good worker because she's Mexican, even though she is Colombian. Since then, Mariana ignored John.

"So, Erika. Your English is very good. When did you immigrate to Canada?" John asks with his forehead wrinkled. I flinch. John's expression stays curious.

"I was born here... in Canada," I say.

John's face is puzzled. "Oh, I see..." He raises his eyebrows and asks, "But where are you *really* from?"

My mouth hangs open.

"You mean, where are my parents from?"

"Yeah, sure," John says.

"They're from the Philippines."

"Ah, I knew it!" John says proudly. "You look so familiar I just had to ask."

"Mhmm," I mumble. I walk to the grinder machine and walk away from Old John. He leaves the counter and walks over to the milk counter. I glare at John. He fills his coffee with two creams and one sugar, and sits by the fireplace.

Five minutes later, Mariana returns from her break.

"Hey Mariana," I say. "Old John just came by. Guess what the hell he asked me."

"Oh no. What did he say?" she asks.

I tell Mariana the whole encounter.

"I mean, what does 'Where are you really from' even mean, you know?"

"Oh my goodness," Mariana laughs. "I can't believe he said that."

Two days later, I go to work at 3:00 p.m. I'm working with Shaina this time. Shaina's a sweet 28-year-old Filipina girl, who has worked for Jim for over three years, and is passionate about latte art. Shaina and I close together at 11:00 p.m. tonight. That means eight more hours of standing around, wiping the same counter four times, and triple-checking full milk cartons by the counter.

In the mornings, Mavis is busy. Ten cars form a line outside the drive-thru. Most customers order a double-double coffee and sometimes they add in a chocolate chip banana muffin or cheddar croissant. Meanwhile, inside the café, two old folks sit on the sofas reading the paper. For the rest of the day, only five people come to the store every hour, and most of them are regulars.

Old John walks in and we go through the regular routine. Today he wears a white golf shirt and khaki shorts. I walk to the coffee machine, pour his medium dark roast, and toss in a few ice cubes. Shaina is by the dining area wiping down tables and changing the empty milk cartons. I cash out John's coffee and glide over to the breakfast area to fix the cheddar croissants on the tray. John follows me.

"So, Erika," he says. "You've been working here a lot. Are you still in school?"

"Yeah, I am. But I'll be back in September after summer break."

"That's great. What are you studying?"

"I'm studying communications and business at the University of Toronto."

"But since you're Filipino, shouldn't you be studying nursing?" John asks.

My smile drains from my face.

"No," I say with a blank stare. "I'm not good with math and science."

"Oh, okay. I just thought you would be."

I breathe deeply. I shuffle next to the coffee machines and organize a tray of dark grey coffee sleeves. I adjust my headset and tap on the button to see if any customers are in the drive thru. John continues the conversation and starts talking about how his daughter graduated from York University from their Schulich program. I peek at the entrance of the café to check for new customers. I nod my head occasionally and pick on a hangnail on my finger.

A few customers walk through the door and wait in line. A wide-eyed couple stands in front of the cake display and point at the Red Velvet cake. A woman with a cane and her eight-year-old grandson ponder over the new Chocolate Strawberry FroCho.

John glances behind him and sees the other customers, but he continues to yap away. I continue nodding at Old John's comments. Shaina comes from the barista machine to help grandma and her grandson. I walk away from John and greet the Red Velvet couple.

"Hello! Welcome to Second Cup. What can I get for you?" I say.

My eyes dart back at John, who is standing beside the couple.

"Well, bye Erika," he says. "That was a nice chat we had today. See you tomorrow!"

I nod.

I repeat John's questions in my head and shudder. I wonder what smart remark he will have tomorrow.

happy bday anna ✿

The room is dark. The only light in the room is twenty-one candles, illuminating Anna's face. Her high cheek bones are carved out from the beaming light.

Everyone in the room sings the birthday song.

She blows out the candles and the room goes dark. The scent of burning wax travels across the kitchen. Someone flicks the light on. I blink hard and my eyes adjust, fixating on Jonathan standing beside the light switches. Jonathan is Anna's boyfriend. They met last year through a friend and have been living together and smoking tons of shisha ever since.

This year for Anna's birthday, she decided to host a pre-drinking party at her and Jonathan's condo before going clubbing downtown at Cube. Anna invites her closest friends to the pre: our best friend Sam and friend Christine. Since Jonathan doesn't have many friends, Anna let him bring his best friend, Lucas, his brother, Nathan, and Nathan's friends.

I've met Lucas a handful of times. Anna would invite me for shisha with Jon and Lucas at Karnak every few months. We hung out and played Crazy 8's or Cheat. Lucas would smack the table when he lost, flexing his biceps.

I arrive at Jon's place. He introduces me to his brother Nathan. He is tall and lanky, jeans sagging, and wears an oversized black polo shirt. Nathan introduces me to the guy next to him, Malik. He has deep skin, tight curly hair, and wears a similar outfit to Nathan's, with a few silver chains hanging around his neck.

Next to Malik, is their other friend, Karim, also wearing a baggy Ralph Lauren polo shirt, with two glistening studded earrings on both ears, and wavy hair gelled back like Zac Efron in Hairspray.

Anna slices her cake, takes a paper plate, and slaps on a slice. The white icing droops to the edges. We pass the slices of cake to everyone around the room. Sam sits beside me, licking the icing off first, with leftovers around her mouth. Christine stands in front of the oversized mirror in the living room, checking herself out.

Earlier in the night, the four of us girls went to Popular Pizza to pick up food before we start drinking. We walked behind the condo, and gossiped since we haven't seen each other since summer.

"How are you and Jon, doing?" Sam asked Anna.

"We're good, just so annoying. We kept fighting today, but we made up."

"Oh no, it's your birthday too," I said.

"I know, so annoying. Like, not today Jon," Anna said.

We all laugh.

"So, Christine, what have you been up to?" I said, "It's been way too long."

"Girl, I know! I work at the Premium Outlets now. I'm in school for nursing," she said, pulling down her skirt to fix it.

"Yo, you guys! I forgot to tell you. Nathan told Jon that his friends thinks you guys are cute." Anna laughed.

"Oh my God, really? Which ones?" Sam rolled her eyes.

"They're both ugly, anyways Sam." Christine smirked.

"I don't know man, but I know Karim thinks you're cute, Erika," Anna said.

"Oh God, what the hell," I replied.

"But don't worry, I got you. I already told all of them you

have a boyfriend," she said.

I laughed. "Alright, thanks girl."

After dessert, the drinking begins. Anna removes four bottles of liquor from the paper LCBO bags. She takes out a bottle of Patron, a bottle of Smirnoff Vodka, and two cases of Heineken.

"Let's take shots!" Anna says pouring the vodka into nine red plastic shot cups. All of us gather in a circle, ready to raise our shots.

"Happy birthday, bitch!" Sam giggles, as we smack our cups together. Whiskey swirls around the edges and splashes on the floor before I force the alcohol down.

"We love you, Anna!" Christine says.

"Happy birthday, baby!" Jon says grabbing Anna's waist and kissing her on the cheek.

Five shots later, we order a couple of Ubers to downtown Toronto. We arrive to Cube at 11:15 p.m. just before we had to pay for cover. Nine of us go behind the bottle service line-up and wait for the bouncer to check our IDs. A handful of stumbling, intoxicated women trip on their four-inch heels while waiting in the line next to us.

We enter Cube. My eyes adjust to the dim space. I spot

a few lights dangling around the room, shining above each booth. Men in sweat-stained blue dress shirts are draped across the bar. The bartender's cleavage gleams under the dark room. A lady in a tight two-piece, like the bartender, brings us to our booth across the speakers.

The whole night, I dance with Sam and Christine. We fist pump to every EDM song, twerk to every Drake song, and sing along to the 90's throwbacks. The guys Whipped and Nae Nae-d in the booth, while pouring more Hennessy in their mouths.

Halfway through the night I sit on the leather booth. Christine left, Anna is dancing with Jon, and Sam is dancing with Lucas. My sweaty thighs stick as I adjust my position on the seat. I take off my heels and rub the edges of my swollen feet.

Nathan and Karim sit on the opposite side of the booth, drinking their glasses of Hennessy. None of them look or talk to me. Malik drinks from the bottle. He could barely keep his eyes open.

At 2:00 a.m. an hour before the club closes, we head back to the apartment.

Jon's living room has no furniture in it, so they blew up three air mattresses for everyone to sleep on. One for me and Sam, and the other two to share for the boys. Anna brings out a few blankets and pillows and heads to the bedroom where her and Jon are sleeping.

I slip on my extra-large, pen-stained, Sam Smith concert tee and grey joggers, after washing up for bed. I walk over to the balcony beside the living room. Sam and Lucas are sitting outside and smoking cigarettes.

"Sam, I'm heading to bed now. It's almost 4:00 a.m. are you coming?"

"Yeah, I'll be there. I'm just going to chill for a bit and have another smoke."

"Alright, night. See you then, Sam. Night Lucas!"

"Night, Erika."

The sliding door creaks as I struggle to close it. I plop myself on the empty air mattress, leaving space for Sam to sleep beside me. Malik and Nathan sleep on the mattress next to me. Karim sleeps across from them with space for Lucas. I wrap the blanket around me, fluff my thin pillow, and pass out.

A few hours later, I feel something moving underneath my blanket. Half asleep, I reach for the thing moving and try to pull it away. It retracted and gripped tighter.

My eyes jolt like I missed my alarm, and was late for my first day of school.

I realize the thing moving, under my blanket, was

someone's hand.

I feel their fingers touching my vagina.

I try to pull away a second time and feel the slither of their arm run across my lower body. They took their hand out from my underwear. I feel weight on the other side of the air mattress, next to me.

My heart thumps in my ears. Every muscle in my body is numb. I don't move anything but my eyes as I try and scan the bodies around me.

Nathan and Malik sleep on the mattress beside me. I see the balcony light on and hear Sam and Lucas still murmuring. I glance over at Karim's bed.

Empty.

I realize I haven't exhaled since I opened my eyes. I let out a breath. I stand up abruptly, and calmly walk straight to the balcony.

I rub my eyes still trying to wake up and process everything. Gripping the black handle of the sliding door, I slide it open with ease.

"Hey, what's up? Why are you guys still up?" I say, looking at Sam and Lucas, still sitting the same way I left them a few hours ago.

"Hey, Erika. Why are you still awake? We're just chilling,"

Lucas replies.

"Oh, just woke up. Couldn't really sleep," I say, sliding the door behind me.

I sit down on the cold, prickly concrete floor with them.

I spend the rest of the early morning on the balcony with Sam and Lucas. I watch their mouths move in slow motion. I hear a ringing noise. The same ring as if you're by yourself in your room at night, listening to the silence.

I nod and smile, pretending to follow along to their conversation. I replay what happened in the living room in my head over and over again.

I replay the fluttering of my eyes waking up and removing something from my pants. I replay the grip of his hand grabbing me. I replay realizing what the fuck was going on.

On the concrete is a thin blanket that Sam used when it got cold during the night. I try to close my eyes and curl up in fetal position to sleep as, Sam and Lucas kept talking. They smoke another cigarette together.

Around 7:00 a.m. Lucas leaves to go to the washroom.

"Why don't you sleep back inside?" Sam asks.

I stare at her. I could feel my eyes burning.

"I-I'm good…" I stutter. "Sam… I need to tell you something."

"Yeah?"

"Umm… well, I woke up in the living room with Karim's hand down my pants…"

"Ew, what the fuck?!" Sam's lip quivers.

"Yeah… I didn't know what to do."

"Are you okay? Want me to go in there and beat the fuck outta him?"

"Nah, that's okay. Thanks so much though," I half-smiled. "I don't even want to think of it right now."

"That fucking disgusting pig. I'll kill him right now if you want me to."

I wanted to pretend it never happened. I wanted to erase my memory like Jim Carrey in *Eternal Sunshine of the Spotless Mind*.

Lucas comes back from the washroom.

Although it is late September, the morning was warm. The air is crisp. I look around the scenery outside the balcony. Cloudy skies. Small green trees stagger below. I see the empty intersection of Eglinton Avenue and Erin Mills Parkway. No people. No birds chirping. No cars honking. The eeriness of the quiet was comforting and abnormal at the same time.

I try to breathe in the morning air, but a lump is caught in my throat. My breathing is uneven. I couldn't inhale the fresh air.

Around 9:00 a.m. I text my mom to pick me up, so I could go home and get ready for work.

"Sam, can you come inside with me to get my things? My mom is on her way."

"Yeah, of course."

I go back inside the apartment. The air smells like body odour and alcohol. I try to avoid looking at the air mattress, but I glance over. Karim is still lying down on my mattress. I slowly creep by the side of the bed to get my glasses, avoiding to step on the roach nearby.

Sam glares at him, like she just smelt the football hallway after practice from high school. Sour, foul, and acidic.

Karim's eyes are shut, his mouth open, and he snores loudly.

"That fucker is faking it," Sam whispers. "When I went inside earlier he asked me to turn the light off."

"Let's just leave."

Sam takes the elevator with me and brings me down to the lobby.

"Can you please tell Anna what happened later? I don't want to text her this…"

"Yeah. Don't worry, I'll tell her for you."

After work, I check my phone to see messages from Anna and Sam in our group conversation.

Anna texts:

Erika, I'm so, so sorry what happened. I fucking cried when Sam told me...

I'm telling Jon to talk to him, he's so disgusting.

I wish you told me Erika, I would've let you sleep in the bedroom with us.

Thanks, Anna I wanted to tell you in person but I had to go. He's fucking gross... I'm just freaking out on telling Mark about this. I can't believe this happened...

Few days later, Mark and I hang out in my room after a long day at work. We lay down on my bed, talk about our day, how work is going, and how our weekends went. I mention Anna's birthday party. Catching up with Sam and Christine, drinking at Cube, and how the music was bumpin'.

"I have to tell you s-s-omething..." I stutter.

"What? Did you cheat on me or something?" Mark asks.

I laugh. "Shut the hell up, no."

I clear my throat and tell him the same story I told Sam.

After speaking, a few tears roll down my damp face. I stare

at him. He doesn't look at me. I follow his eyes staring at the ceiling.

"Are you okay?" I ask.

"Yeah, I'm just glad you're okay. None of this is your fault."

I nod.

"Listen babe," he pauses. "I don't want you fucking hanging out with any of them ever again."

I nod again and wipe the tears trailing my cheeks.

The same cloudy hues from the balcony shine through the sheer white sheets in my room, complimenting my muted blue walls. He wraps his arms around me and wipes my face.

"I'm sorry this happened to you. But you're okay now. None of this is your fault."

We stay in the comfortable eerie silence as he tightens his arms around me. It feels like it's 6:00 a.m. when it was already 7:00 p.m. I listen for the usual train passing by or kids playing outside through the open window. But there was only silence. No people. No birds chirping. No cars honking. Just the same comforting eeriness.

For so long I had trouble putting my thoughts into words
I always wanted to be well liked
So, I would never really tell you how it is
Even though I thought it

It took me a while to feel brave and confident enough
It took me a while to let you know

So, just wait on it
Keep improving, progressing, learning

Keep speaking up

Because endings really are the some of the best parts

thank yous

To my friends and family. Thank you mom, dad, and my sister. Thank you to my boyfriend, Mark, for continuously being my back bone in the entire process of my book.

Thank you so much to everyone for the overwhelming amount of support and love. It really kept me going and helped me stay motivated. I am undeserving of your love!!!

To my writing professors, Guy, Robert, Laurel, and Rahul, for pushing us forward and helping us produce our best work. To my amazing editing groups that have helped me de-stress and edit.

To my fabulous copyeditor, Matthew, for helping me put together this book. I value your patience and intellect. You're amazing.

To my crazy talented friend, Caroline, for the lovely floral, botanical illustrations.

Thank you. Thank you all.

about erika

Erika is a writer, event planner, and unicorn-lover. She was raised in Ontario, Canada and her parents immigrated in the 90's from the Philippines.

She spends days working, volunteering, and watching Netflix. Erika loves attending live shows, planning events, and eating carbs.

Keep updated on Instagram, @SpeakUpErika.

Made in the USA
Columbia, SC
17 June 2018